OFTEN FANGED LIGHT

Often Fanged Light

Poems
by

ANCA VLASOPOLOS

Adelaide Books
New York / Lisbon
2019

OFTEN FANGED LIGHT
Poems
By Anca Vlasopolos

Copyright © by Anca Vlasopolos
Cover photograph © Anca Vlasopolos
Cover design © 2019 Adelaide Books

Published by Adelaide Books, New York / Lisbon
adelaidebooks.org

Editor-in-Chief
Stevan V. Nikolic

All rights reserved. No part of this book may be reproduced in any manner whatsoever without written permission from the author except in the case of brief quotations embodied in critical articles and reviews.

For any information, please address Adelaide Books
at info@adelaidebooks.org
or write to:
Adelaide Books
244 Fifth Ave. Suite D27
New York, NY, 10001

ISBN-10: 1-949180-87-5
ISBN-13: 978-1-949180-87-9

Printed in the United States of America

For Harriet

May the light ever shine gently upon you

Contents

Near the Unnamed Great Lakes 13

Lemons, Before and After 15

Venice on Lake St. Clair 16

Short Silence 17

High-Sky Dis/Pleasures 18

A Lot More than Half Way 19

Cleansing the Haunted House 20

Love Poem to the L(ibrary) before IT 22

Deserving Further Study 24

Another Planet Roll 26

Faithful Facsimiles 27

The Black Beneath 29

as we drove north 31

Nurseryman 33

Bulletin 34

Late Dog Walk 35

Along the Sidewalk 36

Habitats 37

Extreme Weather 38

Final Solutions Revisited. 40

How Much This Song. 42

Making Tender 44

Endings 47

Flash Forward 50

Picking the Ready One 52

Broken Vector 54

Opal Moon 55

as date approaches 56

Summer Blues 58

Why Should 59

Woman in Black in a Locked Garden 61

Stay of Execution 63

Farewell the Roses. 65

Year-End Ornaments 67

Coming to Light. 68

Dance of the Needles 70

at this late date 71

Kitchen Window Still Life 72

Spring Come 73

On Lumbert Pond 75

    Amphibian Landings 77

    This Floating World 78

    Gust 79

    November in Eastern Standard Time 80

    Squalls 81

    Lion-Toothed Lamb 83

    March This Year 84

    Storm Effects Summer's End. 85

    On the Horizon 86

    The Other Solstice 87

    Autumn's Bouquet 88

    If You're Not There All Along 89

    Yes, and Yet. 90

    Aerogrammes 91

    Past Rising 92

    Ghost Owl 93

    Virtual Spaces 94

    October Underside 95

    On Other Days. 96

    Encryption 97

    January's Small Mercies. 98

Unrest of Migrant Selves................99

Song No More 100

Meditation on Gray's Beach 101

Alight.............................103

Migration Eve.......................104

Granddaughter Becoming at Full Moon....105

New Yet Again 107

Horizons Limitless.........................109

Beach Tales......................111

Cape Cod Log 113

Water Writ on Us..................116

Tonight Midsummer 117

Why in Our Age....................119

Paris Sediments...................121

Snailing to (Perchance) Byzantium........123

In This Dark Season 124

December Deeps 126

Inside the Polar Vortex 127

Dog Reading Ocean Beach.............128

Fall Clearance.....................129

Fast Falling......................130

Punishing Weather..................131

MAN in Nature 132

Wake 134

Gratitude 135

Avis Semper Rara 136

In Darkest Hours 137

Acknowledgments............................139

About the Author..........................141

Near the Unnamed Great Lake

Lemons, Before and After

it never made lemons because
    she says
I ate the flowers
I couldn't help it
they taste so sweet

    assuaging guilt
        though she seems not to feel it   merely amused
        at her misdeed
I say
    that poor scraggly indoor tree
    has loads of flowers
    can only keep
        one or two fruit a year

    one daughter takes the lemon   with her lens
    can stay the cutting in
first makes of it a jewel   in still life

the other
starved Mayan child forever pummeling from within
voraciously consumes
        unfurled promises

Venice on Lake St. Clair

the water venetian glass of merchant Dogi
who needn't have counted silver for its burnishing

boats caught as if in ice
reflection so still they become Siamese watertwins

this sun for once serene unbloodied
glides over the marina's captive surface

like those phenomena
the single figure skaters we watch in awe

flashing now this blade the other
into dazzled eye

yet under this window of double plenitude
this June evening calm

devouring mouths seek on
at depths the skeletons langorously comb

black waters' curly currents
with their long phalanges

Short Silence

there is no human sound
    for a brief few seconds
only leaves trailing their rust taffeta hems
    over cement

wind makes a conch
    of my left ear
and I can hear the pounding surf
    elsewhere than here

St. Clair wavelets chasing   chasing
    each other's shoulders
like alewives running
    toward the sea

broken sky   sun in shards
    sends rays at angles
so precise as if a god
    from a lesser-known painting

of the Renaissance
    directed
above clouds
    this late-november show

High-Sky Dis/Pleasures

sun sends
adieus fiery
    one moment
    off white-sided boat
gentle like melting mangoes
    next

while on a lake just hinting
at restlessness
under her gaze
this waxing moon
deigns
only to image
herself
as cut-up
phosphorescent
worm

A Lot More than Half Way

     in our dark woods
notches on trees   aluminum tabs nailed
tell us

     from here on
you're on the path of the orphan
     here
you lose your best love
     here
a leg   a knee   one or more of your senses

     as we crawl on
we grow thankful
     for the small mercies
half a day's
sun

Cleansing the Haunted House

break the cobwebs
    they'll stick and you'll try and try to rid
    yourself of filaments   clinging on as if for dear life

    in this corner
there's
        not ectoplasm
instead   a murder of crows you raise as you break
    through rotten draperies
they'll go for the eyes

    weeping furious tears
you swipe at them
catch most   you hope   between covers
    contain though you cannot
    quite kill them

    old loves   long gone   the love or those who loved
        whisper to you anew from crumbling leaves
those too you must
    give rest to

    damaged shutters obscuring light
        triumphs no less than griefs

OFTEN FANGED LIGHT

you send to become pulp reincarnated
  to root in other brains

wipe away layers
   particles that still utter their small shrieks

look now
   the roll-top desk
     so clean like a change purse
  ready to shut with an emphatic snap
    upon its guarded essences

Love Poem to the L(ibrary) before IT

you who carry the world in your palm
the weighty equivalence of Alexandria's wisdom
inside a slender electronic case
may never know

how we who trespassed among the isles
    where one winked wickedly
    another flashed a sumptuous jacket
    yet another drunkenly sideways
    stared us down
    amused

fell for
most often a quickie
an all-nighter
sometimes
were rendered captive
for a lifetime
by a spine
cracking open
waving leaves in breezes
like the anemone
in deep-sea raptures

that one
a potter because a Japanese
book of cookery's aesthetic
oddment of finery for food display
consumed him
that other
mounting the ladder
of terza rima
through hell
high water
to Paradise

Deserving Further Study

they stripped us of valuables they called them
    a gold charm   a fur collar   what else would we have
    if even these   worse
they stripped us of what
    bound together the scattered leaves of days—
        books photographs anything handwritten
        beat-up toys
they felt for   then tore the hem
    of travel dresses   broke up chocolate packs
        forbade peeled oranges
they unbirthed us
forced us to uncitizen ourselves   loosed us—penniless
    with a stamped beggar's sheet of paper—on the
    unwilling world

but   god   it felt so good to be unyoked in youth!
    that sheet my flying carpet

the U. N. took the paper
    tsked its collective head   issued cardboard
    passes crossed by a line of red like signs prohibiting
        "refugee   stateless"

for years I exulted
>   on every application   "Citizen of what country?"
>   none

then threads   mesmeric   invisible   wove me down
>   held me here   where I am   my passport solid
>   respectable   a navy man to steer me by the elbow
>   on perilous seas

I read that they now publish a journal of refugees
>   no   not for
they even said they let
>   refugees speak of themselves
>   in the first issue

Another Planet Roll

      each passing roll
trees
      readying themselves for the uncompromising severity of
      winter
shed baubles   bangles
plaster the dark cement with lipstick-stained letters
          adieu   adieu

      and even on this full-heartedly clement late-October day
sun's slant
      as early as three pm
tells us
truth

Faithful Facsimiles

they must have cost a ton
these plaster figures   three magi   the mother   her protector
          all kneeling
and the swaddled baby   outsized   in his strange cocoon

they're from a time when no one minded a black face with a turban
     a lighter but still dark
         and then a blond   just like mother and child

the paint is not intact
there're chips on edges of scalloped clothes and veils

they come whence antecedents of these inhabitants
     of the vast manse two steps from the lake
must have begun their upward climb

each Christmas season on the vast stone terrace of this
immense pile
     ten bedrooms two drawing rooms two conservatories
     grounds to keep crews at making noise all summer
the plaster figures take their place
announcing worn pieties   allegiances half-remembered

by the   ever-blonder   cooler   less gesticulating descendants
    of those taste-impaired folk who bought such
    declarations of newly moneyed faith

    and as I walk this nearly deserted street where rarely
    children play
I contemplate the chances now   today
    of pity from owners invisible behind their hundred
    windows
        for the unwed Jewess and her brat
    their hospitality to those dark   weirdly clad
        readers of firmament

The Black Beneath

sea monsters
    they say now
wore black   no exception
        the sole reminder   leatherback turtles   and they
           on their way out

black
    they say
        well adapted for warmth in frigid seas
           now going to soup
black
    they say
        melanin to keep lithe creatures
           from burning up

so those drawings on early oceans
    the naïf cartographers   ever so much sillier than all-
    knowing we

black serpents with heads of dragons
    flukes
        shark teeth
you tell us

Anca Vlasopolos

did they not rise
     from our first   water   sights
were they not
        what broke through thin layer
            of our leviathan
fears?

as we drove north

from gentle weather
trees still waving
flame-colored handkerchiefs
in their farewell to summer
daughters   cousin   friends
sweet evenings of communion

from an October still
harboring some hope

we passed the Pennsylvania hills
        only a week before vying with sunsets
        in autumnal beauty
    now swept near bone
    by rain and wind storm
moved through Ohio where we still
saw stragglers of the last rally
before the hope of sanity was killed

came into Michigan
    November
    skeletal vegetation
    election day 2010

Anca Vlasopolos

our descent
into the maws
of that vise
small days
frost
general over this land

Nurseryman

He's young and black and carrying bags
    of dirt   manure   chips   sand to open
    trunks
dumps them
    his spite against their weight
        and the leisure of those who've got nothing better
        to do than dump them somewhere in their yards
not thinking   maybe thinking too hard   how if
        they didn't he wouldn't
        have to haul these back-breaking
        bags he calls "bitch" and "motherfucker"
or maybe he calls the people buying them or those
    who pay him at best minimum wage by these names
        leaving   genderraceclass   behind
he having been borne above   beyond these nice
distinctions
        by the greater swell and gust of a job
        not merely dead-end
        deadening
    but one that sees you
        dead

Bulletin

yesterday the sun teethed
baby gums of summer now bared
serrated crests
gripping the leaf to blood
splintering light
to leave the eye in tears

last night a frost told us the bite was on

today hoodlum winds
rip
pointed dutch bonnets
off milkweed pods
silken hair streaked with seeds
     released
blows where
it might

Late Dog Walk

    on barely lit streets
shadows pursue   grow to grotesque dimensions

leaves on wet pavement
    curled into themselves as if from cold
shine
    carapaces of ancient insects
        armored
    come to take back the earth

Along the Sidewalk

leaves on the privet hedge
        punched
        knocked about
        by this ruffian wind
bruised
to yellow purple
yet clinging on

then
wind
brings in
thug chills

overnight they tear off
stragglers too long
        now lying
        dry
        curled
        corpses
        on top
        the down counterpane
        of snow

Habitats

    in dreams only
you come back
say
    hanging another ton weight to my guilt
    why did you give away my clothes   my everything?
how will I live
    and that longtime companion grief wakes   lashes me

what shall I say
spotted- and striped-chested birds
    as they return
    to what they've known as haven for millenia
    now three backyards' worth
look   now only two
soon to be only one

and
    inevitably as I leave for my own haunting grounds

none

Extreme Weather

you at least only rarely shock me
                with romance

    after brute tearing by mad winds
        heaving waters of sky   oceans   tributaries
      upon so many

    even here in the upper midwest where
        the hem of Sandy's mantle swept off the lights

    after the great wrench of another election
        cracking this nation like a whacked coconut

the faraway daughter   the closeaway daughter
    my friend   i
got sucked
    into this mellifluous mildness
    not wholly masking needle teeth
        worrying us from beneath
fell for this gift of mid-november day
    weirdly tingeing with tender breath
        these last hanging leaves
            left blushing
        these last flitters

OFTEN FANGED LIGHT

        for they
                better than we
know
tomorrow we will huddle
     like snails from jibes
     in our sole casings
         against cold
             against loss

Final Solutions Revisited

benign, grandmotherly,
blue eyes behind bifocals

focus
like pinprick scanner

voice
slightly accented in a good Nordic way

rises
"the deer—they starve to death

a pity
kill them

and feed
them to the indigent"

rises again
"the geese poop over the picnic grounds
so dirty

kill and feed them
to the indigent"

OFTEN FANGED LIGHT

in mind's eye
see the indigent

facing a hunk
of tough deer sinew

stringy muscle-tight
goose wing

watch as they wince
"mama, do I gotta eat?"

in mind's ear
grandmotherly slightly accented

voice rises
kill them

and feed them
to the deer and geese

How Much This Song

at the corner Mexican restaurant
in Santa Barbara
the mariachi band appareled in black and silver
featured a round-faced little boy
turning his whole body
inside out
aiiaiiaiiai
aiiaiiaiiaiii
then saying as the band made the rounds
ten dollars for a song

it seems an age
you in the back seat
      the cassette from the Smithsonian that we bought you
      so you'd have home music in your strange new home
      turning for the eleventh time
sang tunelessly
aiiaiiaiiai
aiiaiiaiiaiii
while I blind in the summer storm
tried hard to keep us from ending
in Lake Erie
then Lake Chautauqua

my story of our journey I offered then
for joyous laughs
    you oblivious wrapped in your songs
        utterly trusting that I'd steer us through

now all I hear is but
    llorar llorar llorar
the chorus
mockingly
urging
me to grieve

Making Tender

here
years upon years
they strike not
deadly
blows
just swift ones
at the shins
the ribs
they skewer
a small
perhaps not vital
organ
now and then

in-laws
let in
to body
brain
by cruel
cannibal rites
of wedded bliss

there
where the Cross looms as big
as Andes peaks
not in memory
of wrath
against
those who smite orphans
but as prison bars
—the hidden face of bliss—
shutting
in
small girl
in father's house crawling with underfoot tots
awaiting
in dread and knotted love
his hands
his pocket knife
to carve so gently
his brand
indelible
on her small olive belly
marking
his ownership
so she
will
never
break
from
wanting

Anca Vlasopolos

only
this
and yet
what are they thinking?
spirit will gnarl
may break
but
only dead meat gets tenderer with blows

Endings

this is not the way
the story
inevitably
goes
this is the route
no one
is better for reading
the no
happy
no
moral
no
feel-
good
ending

in this one
I am Hades
not Demeter
though each
might strike
us
as mere chess masters

moving
pawns
the Queen
to the predictable tune—
their own longing

yet in this one I stand
not for desire
only
for
abyss
torment
rack of my will
silent screams
shades
parading
grotesque
wounds
as warnings

above
    where the daughter
    imagining herself
    kidnapped
    thinks
    light
    summer
    ripe fruit hanging from boughs
there
is

no
Demeter
only
unbridled
want
howling
like a pack
in midwinter
for
her
tender
unwise
already so scarred
flesh

Flash Forward

the car still running in the wintry night
i run to open the door to the garage

motion sensor tears open
driveway sagging gate tracery of ivy

inside this cave where i intend to park
a figure camouflaged in shadows

strikes the spotlight thrown on the back wall
     stands huddled   head like turtle hidden

from this boulder-cracking cold
heart pounding i call out

your Mayan olive face   obsidian eyes
peer out from fringe of black hood

you're pale and wan and trembling
i long to gather you into my arms

but that is the last thing you want
you want the fifty bucks to take you off

OFTEN FANGED LIGHT

from who knows what misery
and as i shudder in sympathy with you

something you also do not want
i wake so tightly wound that i might break

Picking the Ready One

my mother said the skin needs to be taut   not tight
    and very red— never gone off to burgundy
the tuft   all that's left of a flower that I've never seen
    dry and erect like clean fur
that's where you can tell—
    if puffs like smoke rise as you stroke it
beware of rot inside

I show my daughter over a large plate:
you make four incisions   quartering it into the elements
it will bleed on your fingers   the blade   the plate   clean
    red that stains indelibly
so watch your clothes
    and table linens
        as you tear open
the sphere will spill out seeds like salmon eggs
    crimson translucent held by a membrane you'll
        crunch between your teeth
your mouth will fill with sweet asperity
    tongue play with kernels exposed like embryos
        outside their amniotic sac
you may spit them out

in fall we must go shopping for pomegranates

    if we can teach each other about this fruit ripened for
    the dry season
        a camel keeping a reservoir inside
then Hades can gnash hysteric among the shades
go fuck himself
        as we drink   feed   on our shared blood

Broken Vector

in this october rich with thrushes
speckling the grass
rusting already crumbling light
with tail flicks

i think of you
my young daughter
migrant
whence these birds winter

you sheltered reluctant
as wild bird in cage
with us for eight years
fretting at the inordinate season

did everything to make your flight
inevitable
so now we wonder
once we've taken our last journey
if you'll one late resplendent fall

again arrive

Opal Moon

> *October child, Christopher Leland, in memoriam*

    the evening after your death
a crescent moon just cleared the rooftops
        translucent
        petal of spent lily

heat hung low
the dog and I pushing through the cottonwool

    when we turned back
the moon
        risen
glittered
    with brassy conquering light
        we   left below
        groped our way
    darkling

as date approaches

for Bella Gad, in memory

I

i recall your voice over the wires
(do we talk across wires anymore? or do our words now
bounce among the stars?)
across a sea and ocean and continent for certain

you told me of your aches   body's and heart's
i (silent as to the other) said i ache too from my fall
you said   not like this

and i expected as many times before
you to reply
     wait till you get my age to know what pain is

but this time
     how would i know it would be our last
you said for once   as if in benediction

     your old age may be kinder than mine is

II

incendiary sky consuming
but itself
going
in only two blocks' walk
to grey

    from falling gloom
       brown   silent   this shape
do we ever know the shape souls take   track their migration?
      trajectory so low
          it nearly hits my forehead
              like a hat tossed in joy

swallowed
the next second
by foliage turning black

Summer Blues

and so it blooms again
    bursts of stars on ends of crosswires
chicory you loved
    profligate   hanging on to road sides

    with amber eyes and honey hair
you looked resplendent in its color
the chicory dress clothed you for that last time
but I could not bear to have them crack the coffin open

    now each summer road
    punctuated by these blue flowers
awakens me to you inhabiting that dress

    o so alive

Why Should

the shredded silk lining
    of these fawn gloves
    I throw on picnic bench as I unleash the dog after our
    walk
hit me
as if the traveler before me thoughtlessly let go
    a branch
    whipping across my face
leave me
    staggering

it's been
    I try to calculate
    while the dog romps among the fallen leaves
oh more than forty years
    easily forty five
        since you brought me this find
            long elegant fawn gloves
    to go with my so dear suede coat

it's been
    not hard to calculate
twenty-three years   a month   ten days

Anca Vlasopolos

since your body lay in such abandoned sleep
    that you could nevermore hear and come to give
comfort to my screamed grief

Woman in Black in a Locked Garden

at your "life and resurrection"
        death it appears no longer a PC word in church
your dog
    like me
makes ready to bolt

priests enter in their frocks intoning their *ple*atitudes

I run   think I may have   as times before
    to loiter in the parking lot
but here
    by bearing left   I find myself
        in a small dusty garden
          a few beds tended with precision
      iron gates padlocked against unlikely passerby

in my good clothes
I do the humble gardener's chores
    squash aphids from the roses
    freeing these buds for their one effulgence
a bird alluring flits in the chestnut whose chandeliers this hot
May are already spent
    —common sparrow twirling in glamour of relentless
    light—

while sun burns
swallows rush into a sky unmarred
    shout their chitterings to hear each other above roar
    of the wounded city

I return to cavernous musty pile
    in time to hear
        your soul's child sob over the hole
        your death shot through her life
    my ears ringing with screamed twitters
        green-thumbed

Stay of Execution

i want it   the power
        to order it

since already
        not yet mid-august
spiderwort closes tight
          green fists
           over violent flowers
      already
evening primrose tinges
        leaves scarlet
rose hips
        begin their slow burn

i deadhead
        forbidding these rebels
          their subversive underground urge

keep at it
      i command
      and they send
        one
          each day
            more dispirited
      sexshop

        while bees
            instead of their ecstatic rolling
       now sated
            bending the stem
drowse

Farewell the Roses

    when names of friends   like fading stars
        are lost to failing senses
        students' names in droves fall
            lemmings off the cliff of memory

why
do i still remember
names
    of roses planted over twenty years ago

some meaningful   Ingrid Bergman   my mother's face
        that gorgeous symmetry
    World War Two Memorial
      Richie Boy Ralph   your father   your uncle
        all my lost unknown kin

others without much sense
      Abraham Darby   what's he to me
  trite   obvious   English Yellow Rose   Red Ribbon

    on this mid-November Michigan day
i cull the last four
    one a bud   two full-blown doused in exquisite scent
      one just beginning its unfurling

tomorrow they'd be bowed beneath the snow

    inside this vase that'll not survive much longer
they light
    surprised by warmth
        their peach   cream   blood-red
lamps

    one more time

Year-End Ornaments

solstice smashed through this year
    a fist into smoked glass

light sang halleluiahs into our dark-numbed brains

    toward end of shortest day
the sun
    using itself sparingly
poured just a few drops of molten rays

the lake spread them to gold foil

    on nearly foreclosed trees   branches gaping wide
breast plumes of robins glowing
turned all our plaster   plastic   suspended   electrified
attempts
    to summon cheer
tawdry   irrelevant

Coming to Light

      after the winter solstice
            like thoughts kept long in darkness
they begin

      centipedes glued like clumped hair
      move at lightning speed

      spiders consider
           then undeterred
      crawl
           toward goals we can't see

I beg them
stay hidden
the house is empty enough
to hold us all

for
      while I try not to harm
instinct rises
hand swipes at scurrying

    and on the tub wall
a single
filament leg
trembles
    with dolor
    of severing

Dance of the Needles

    this winter
daytime has been as cold as other winters' brittle moonlight
    ready   like icicles   to crack and spear you

    in sunlit but unwarmed air
they dance
    slivers   magnets   glomming on to gold

    watch them
minuscule sabers parrying thrusting
    luminous   anorectic sparks

    thralldom
the ice queen's reign upon all
        death   a ballroom of glittering bone shards
           beckoning

at this late date

I needn't tell you
        angels fall swift like lightning
    their horns   no pleasing Telemann
    roar of stabbed thunder

their nature   though   stays true to ether
    so   jocular   they show white undersides
                jocular
they put knives to the kid's throat
    knowing they won't make the final cut

    while you undone
        can only try a sail   machine   wing sketches
        can only try   mock soar
and live quaking for their descending jokes

Kitchen Window Still Life

Remembering Dorothy Wordsworth

a blink of an eye   a century
           ago
this vine
trumpeted persimmon melodies
     as dazzling as Louie's
       while
hummers probed   balanced on their surgeon needles
        shimmying in emerald sequins
     for aphrodisiac sweets

     at the kitchen sink
i see emptied pods
think of Dolly
     and her desolation   pod forever void

try   try   try
     to imagine under rockhard ground
        each seed wrapped in warm coils of birdshit
            dreaming
cotyledon poised   like a ballerina on one pointed shoe
     for its leap
        to
           spring

Spring Come

overnight
winds they warn you about
tore limbs
        limbs we call them though trees don't walk or hug
now
stuck in snow banks

yet look
at buds
up close

only a week ago
shut fast like bankers' fists

now
softened
red-pink
nipples
raised
to suckle
this
nascent
        sunwarmth

On Lumbert Pond

Amphibian Landings

     on this living mirror
         subtle ripples as if on old glass
you see
a flag   pirate colors
   plant itself white-and-black
   then do its buffle act
here duck   here not a trace of me

you see
first
shapes swift-moving   launched arrows
     then
   cacophony of churning water
    turning to symmetry   circle within circle within circle
as these tough customers
      ten in all   I count them
plunge   giraffe necks black beaks
   into opaque depths
     while their plump pointed backsides
       spear
          skyward

This Floating World

this   hallucination
              terra firma

a sandbar swiss-cheesed by glaciers   their craters
              their wounds still running   clear
          sweet water on this narrow strip
              amid salt   brackish   waves

and   no   you cannot go from here to there
the shortest way is never a straight line

each waterhole   each creek forcing you
              into obeisance
      reminds you
           here   for now
you may not override this scape

each stronger   more violent   storm pounding into you
you're a mere speck
      a fever-bearing tick
            on the planet's skin

Gust

look how it starts
    a few sparse leaves on that branch thinly drawn over the
    water

    beginning to shiver
then a fever shakes the whole slender tree

contagion moves up oak and white pine and pitch pine
    woods sway   moan

    wind   seasoned lover   done now with foreplay
howls too   whipped wild ecstasy

November in Eastern Standard Time

light aslant already on the bay and only one pm

on oceanside water already gilded for late pearlescence
grasses sharpened so silver-fine   they cut the eye

the parking lot crunchy from mollusk shells
dropped at twenty feet
    for herring gulls have learned
      to make our ends their means   so they survive
    with   perhaps us

another   and another   and another week   sailing us
toward dark
stars out at four o'clock
and we   like jays   like peeps   gorging   gorging
in light   the little light

Squalls

in seconds freeway
turned to ballroom
where snow ghosts glided
elegantly in close embrace
swirled
billowing skirts
hypnotically
to metronome
of wipers

on overpass
capricious January
breath
congealed
and of a sudden
ballroom changed
to tableware laid
treacherously
on dance floor
flow-blue
bone
polished
porcelain

show us
we cried
the pattern lovers
in willow
running
getting away
from
ireful snowy father
give us
safe
exit
yet please
keep us
inside this rim

Lion-Toothed Lamb

first sunshine in weeks
and weeks   it seems
this thug winter
last of january

trees strangely full of robins
chickadees   cardinals
    as if in deep spring
pouring forth
drunk
on light
    flashing keen
    blades

March This Year

   floored it into late june
       laid a patch
            green like St. Patrick's beer
                through winter muck

   stunned
scilla daffodils hyacinths forsythia magnolias
rush
    jostle
        fearful they'll miss their one chance a year
   shed covers the way
   we pile comforters in closets
       put away heavy socks gloves

He just as fast
    stomps on brakes   skids   and
    screeches us back into Himself

       leaving our hungers
         splayed
             utterly unclothed

Storm Effects Summer's End

    but for the storm the oriole feeder (you rushed indoors)
        jelly hardening   orioles a week ago gone for the year
would still sway in wind   baffle tapping farewell in Morse
    code on the pole

    but for the storm the large hanging pot (you in a hurry
    took down)
        petunias cascading all the bright days
would still wobble   its charge turned to brown stalks

    but for the storm the humminggirl
        parents gone   brother gone too jewels shot into
        southern space
would not suck at nectar as if this were her last meal

    but for the storm—its name my long-dead mother's—
    pounding
        in my shattered brain   these dancing wires—lit
        electric bursts—
would not blind me   ducks in eel grasses eluding my ocular
pursuit

On the Horizon

you inside
didn't see i'm sure
the march of three symmetrical clouds
across the whole northern horizon
backdrop
lit by an already dropped
sun

and in the by-now welcome
desolation
     coming so very late—past
     halloween—
     grabbing by handfuls
     leaves
     throwing them violently
     into lowered faces
do we find
portents
of our solitude

do we
instead
at last
say
it is over
and
let ourselves
exhale

The Other Solstice

guillotine blade severed seasons
       yesterday
             earth soft enough to plant bulbs

today
    hardened
        down to molten core

diving ducks   thinned to stragglers
perform vanishing acts on closing hands of water

       like a prop
moon pulls herself over the rim
            onionskin letting through lambent sky
         calling to her lover
   sun
       now shredded on these lit branches
           melting pearlescent
              on heaving waves

it is this
    is it not
        barely perceptible
              sliver
      on the empty cakeplate of days
        keeping us
           noses pressed against iceglass
         looking

Autumn's Bouquet

on lawns they spread minute to minute
blooms
like red lips
kissing adieu

    like those
    who get up from their death bed
    to make a fabulous meal
    stitch together
    as they puncture
    our tattered hearts

    soar over our rodent cares
    like raptors
    plunge
    and
        as body hits terrestrial dimension
    breath? perhaps disperses in the breeze

they
like the first hard frost
scatter
on cold ground
our colchicum
hopes

If You're Not There All Along

did I know that they rise
    inquisitive
    breaking surface
    wine-dark like turtle heads

did you know
    they open like serviettes let loose
    from their rings
    fold out into soft plates

did we know
    winds lift green hems
    of spread skirts
    the underside blushing

    between open palms
now a decorative lightbulb popped up
soon   we know   to split like sectioned oranges

float cream chalices unruffled the way we imagine
    if we're not there all along to witness
        chases and bullying
            swans who too appear serene

Yes, and Yet

yes   the farm porch did slant into the house
         long enough to have water eat
             wood that keeps the house afloat

yes   dark materials come out in handfuls from what were
      wall supports

yes   of course it'll cost   and cost

yes   it's all built on nothing but sand after all
         falling fast into the lower half of the hourglass

yet   each day I'm ravished anew

for now the pond offers these lilies up
     white   yellow   porcelain bowls
and water forever calls down sky
sky burnishes image   perpetual narcissus
    hanging over pond's edge

      each hour   Rheims cathedral   veiled in another light
      each hour   chiming from trees' bell towers
         in different melodies   cacophonies
       winged remnants
   warning love

Aerogrammes

      no matter how often but after all not that often
we look in wonder
    at beings of the air leaving behind
        for us   (we want to think)
            a memento   on sand   on sidewalk   in the grass

    sometimes non-descript   light-brown
        like anything: dry leaves   pine needles
    sometimes so bright as if a fabric scrap blown in
           from a Parisian haute-couture salon

look at this wing feather mostly white
        a dash of black   inside a triangle of white
    this tail feather
        black-luminous gold
    this—brash blue
    this one pulling sunsets into minute barbs

    these almost angelic vanes
        benign sheddings   like a hair strand on a sleeve
           a tuft of fur from scratching
        not
the struggle before death in higher talons   the crash
    into a window
(we want to think)

Past Rising

it rises
    wraith of yesteryear
the Cape Cod I remember when in my own late-teen erotic fog

  effulgent early-summer afternoon wreathed
     in grey veils
        a beauty hiding age's wreck

  dog's fur damp
  my hair puffing
      dandelion seedhead

horizon   roads   houses
  swathed
      in moist fluff

Ghost Owl

huge wing drapes itself generously over the fallen tree
i peer through late-january gray

gray clockface grayer outline meets my astonished eyes
i point the camera   its zoom mocked by distance
    by window melting with drops
        by pond's white breath

later   try all the techno tricks
      —enlarge contrast brighten enhance—
a demon with impossibly long horns peers back
    familiar pile i say   downed trunk twisted branches
        re-formed in this oscuro of old and damaged prints

next day in brilliant light i search for face or shape
    among   broken pitted tree bones
        left from time and weather's relentless questionings

    nothing there like what my camera caught
    nothing like that blurred   camouflaged
    great bird

Virtual Spaces

the virtual album opens
       a click at a time
            photos of   perhaps   a city
   i once inhabited
       that once inhabited   me

can i be sure
this allée cathedraled by huge trees is the one
    where we ran wildly through the golden leaves
        gathered lustrous new chestnuts

can i know with any certainty
this bridge generously arching over the park lake is the same
    where my small hoodlum friends and i hung over the
    balustrade
        feet off the ground (our mothers' nightmare)
           to watch through greenish waters
              murky mysterious shapes

    like this holey bridge
        that allée sprinkled with sun almost too glorious to
        withstand
memory lights   then blows out
        its flame

October Underside

now the wind   naughty child   sticks fingers
    under the edge of these plates
    that have served luscious summer
and they throw over the plenty
    showing us blood-dark underside   a warning

lily bowls   too   close up

sun's slant no longer graces our high windows

light melts like French vanilla over the pond
earlier each day
putting us on a cruel diet
    o so brief flambé of trees

On Other Days

crows caw their warnings
glide on fringed hems
torpedo routed hawks
never quite settle   bright-sighted   spear-beaked
    eyeing suspiciously the passerby

    today
clouds fit into each other
    soft belly scales of sky fish
so not a peep of clear light smuggles through

    today
crows hang on treetops
    one   by   separate   one
        ornaments of woe

Encryption

    as so often
crows sound alarms

the pond
    its molten glass held fast
    by myriad lily pads
        making you think
        you might just walk on water
springs into sound   ripples
    with frog leaps

a shadow
    like a small plane
passes

    then soaring above the tallest pines
a hawk
    underside barred and speckled
    an antique music sheet
        scoring a silent song

what must it be like
    to see
        this masterful deployment
            from above?

January's Small Mercies

    only a fingerling of water left
        of pond in winter's vise
yet clown-beaked ducks act
        as if this tiny world were all they needed

Unrest of Migrant Selves

spring is the time for leaving
    may the most dangerous month

        the time when whatever thought of unfurling
finds itself pierced by inexorable claws
      fripperies stripped
          excrescences dropped off

    as body deftly opened
lets go its cling to earth
      pulse   breath   tendon   shocks of neurons

beats   wings
    blind to all holds
        but *zugunruhe**

    wild for flight

*Ornithological term for migratory restlessness

Song No More

    one emerald   three nondescript   beige caterpillars
        beak tight upon them
all
arrested
as unimaginable speed and weight thudded against this
handful
        nothing but fluff
        markings on chest we call a triangle

life gone gives me this close-up   dreadful present

    somewhere nearby
nestlings peep
    for food in beak   now laid on asphalt

crows know their chance

    somewhere nearby

Meditation on Gray's Beach

this boardwalk arching over marsh
    straight to that line we imagine
        between bay and sky
takes me
    into its sensuous cedar arms
keeps me
    from vertigo

        because
look
    down in low-tide grasses
my body
lies on its side
    as if in sleep

the great black-backed gull settles
    above my eyes

crabs scuttle between   then for
    my toes

but I keep walking
    walking

watch me
> go on between these sturdy arms even an ocean gale
> cannot tear asunder

watch
> till you see me
>> no
>>> more

Alight

this should not be news
it may not be for some

they plunge   fiery arrows
with such abandon we think they might dash out tiny brains

this circumscribed world flares   fades
    as these shafts pierce air

agape we watch the coming   the going   of this circus
    flaming acrobats   angels plunging without nets

and know
if we have not dashed out our brains on altars of stupefying gods

    when they're no more
        no more is this   our tenuous hold

Migration Eve

> *For Heather, who showed me*

when the dun breast of young gull gets painted in fire

when barking   screeching angels jostle
     for a hold on this tree suddenly looking
         like nothing so much as illuminations
     for *Tree of Life*

when grubby freight train barrels down into infinity
     sending vanes   shafts into dazzling ascent

when eye   of night heron perched atop tallest pine
     fixes red-hot on the all

     in twilight like this   if there is soul   even a breath
let it take
     from my lips   along with these impossible wings
flight

Granddaughter Becoming at Full Moon

we deny it
    superstition
        we say
yet we see with our own eyes how the beach lies empty of
water
    while moonface looks as if she's swallowed at least a
    couple of seas
and we see how the grasses today at new moon sway in the
high waters
    so high   we ourselves admit   as we've not seen

so how can the frost moon beaver moon not draw out
burst that sac of salt water

how cannot she call to the full child   it too mostly salt water

how can such small bodies of our waters
deny her

thus the frost moon beaver moon beckoned
and you
November moon granddaughter
    crowned with hair catching moonbeams

    fingers splayed like starfish stretching under that glow
opened your mother's body
    wide to Archer goddess
came out to arms open like O's
lifted your lids to feel night pulsing in silver light

New Yet Again

in late may it's still early spring here
where the woodland floors crackle as if
shells of new eggs are all over
breaking
as if
    despite news of yet more oiled birds   beached whales
        fouled beaches
despite the rending we do even here
    of this planet we've so loaded
        with our discards and misery
the world were
bursting open for the first time
and all that unfurls—dragonflies' wings   fronds   leaves—
could turn in wonder
    shining like children's eyes
at my graying progress

Horizons Limitless

Beach Tales

the day whistles past ears
        salt kisses
August sun gentles rhythmic roar   this impartial
           pulse we heard as soon as we began
              that will beat as long as orbits hold

on our towels we are taken
    with imagining you a lover handsome bright
    attentive   of course
        (we don't want him unflawed like a stone)
so we give him small defects
        vain about his beautiful hands
           flashes a tasteful ring to show off
              fine long fingers
we create a Vietnamese son
    his Indochine love affair with a woman
        not nearly so good as you
           but then he was very young
    an artistic somewhat distant mother
    the father a diplomat
    he born to privilege but having learned
        to serve

so taken with making we don't notice the sun
        sneaking under breeze sharp with smells we only
    remember from a time before we could smell
          sun balming salt sand sting of sea wind
    sun quietly licking licking skin
        that tomorrow will furiously blush
so taken we are with the making of a man almost
    good enough for you

Cape Cod Log

Aubade

crow hops in gray light   off balance from the wing
      trembling still in its beak
they scream   the gathering of sparrows and finches,
    as the crow rights itself   vanishes over cedar shingles,
        weathered verdigris of sails and arrows
          piercing sea wind

small birds on wire chirp quietly
crow returns
they let out sharp alarms

later they leave   a few together   one by one
      notes in a minor key descending
        from a piccolo score

Vespers

    under the catalpa trees
she says leaning over the bowl brimming with globe thistles
      phlox fairy roses dahlias
we sit in the long light of July afternoons

    talking politics
and she says
  I must call my brother
    can you smell these
      gesturing to the phlox rising like coral dust
      mops over the bowl
  as children we were sent to brush our teeth under the
catalpa trees
    the phlox were blooming then
father sent us from camp with our little cups
  I must call my brother
    it's not his birthday
      her husband gently mocks
    can you smell these
      she says

Nocturne

  travel pictures again
nothing but the stills stays thirty-years' time
look at this coast for instance
    erosion eating so much of one side
      sand bar houses trees left only in these siftings
        old bricks salt-cured shingles limbs
the tide keeps worrying
    other side so replete the water moves ever farther
      tide pools and flats stretching miles
        pearl sheen in late light
          like remnants finely sanded
         crafted to near transparency

so they glow like treasures with each receding
sigh
  like this still
    taken nine years ago
   double exposed
so mother daughter daughter
 float on the steps of this ethereal building
  translucent
so a wealth of blossoms reaches through brick
    stone muscles cheekbones hands for light

Water Writ on Us

"the worst blizzard on record" could not inscribe
    itself upon the ocean
        lapping
            serene
    a wounded shore

not five days later
      after a night to freeze the marrow in the bone
i see water   intense aquamarine   far to the horizon
    from shore a crust—wetted and reconfigured sugar—
    spread like sheet cake

        yet underneath that green-tinged layer
systolic   diastolic   rhythms   pulse
these miles of winter thrall heave
and we   we   amazed   acknowledge ancient
beat   our incipience
    and   when stilled   our end

Tonight Midsummer

tonight Midsummer
should i traipse through
mosquito-infested grasses
shrub boughs spraying
skin-shivery drops
burr thorn cobweb
for that magic flower
the one
you know
blooming only this once

i have lost touch
with languages of humans
love is a worm-bored gourd
holding nothingness
hatred writhes—a defanged
mangled rattler
used by peddlers of those rocks
called faith

and i forget who cries from foliage
at dawn's shafts

so yes i'll brave
bite scratch lyme disease
to seek the one
that grants me
hearing
to understand
what now i feebly call
tumult
heaving
sighs
murmur
susurration

the words and grammar and syntax
of the trees

Why in Our Age

Wordsworth in his glory
    howled for lost splendour in the grass
        little knowing soon his own flowering would die off

    in his drugged haze
Coleridge rent nature's garment to find only
      rattling   the bones of his dried love

"she gave me eyes, she gave me ears" gave all
    till left hung out to flap
        old seedless pod upon a stick

they   and others like   passed through doors into
eternities of mind
    ever in peril
        for minds do fade like patterns left in sun
and newer minds may not sit down to that full table of the soul

why in our age do we
hear so much more of illness and of death
    instead of weddings   births
      since traffic
    at each portal

must still
      must it not
be brisk

where have they gone
eternities of mind. . . .

Paris Sediments

layered under time
when violently opened
the city shows the depths of our ruin
these chambers   baths   theaters   temples
a time when gallo-roman gamins
could frolic in a Seine
not corseted in banks of stone

layered across my insignificant chronology
she drives in the spike of memory
for all that's gone and flown
since last time and all the times before
I stood on these same stones

acacias flowering out of season
this early august
at every breeze
shed blossoms on our heads
not heeding grey or sparseness

on the boulevard
sycamores
let down

a rattle of dry leaves
reminder
that
despite those stray blooms among our curls
the season
        juggernaut
moves on

Snailing to (Perchance) Byzantium

      as i am crawling toward old age
i try to leave behind my habit(at)
          glorious though it was
              stylus-scored spirals mauve against moss-green
              inscribing all—exuberance   pain   sorrows
              terrors

      at my age
i cannot sail forth like a proud naked muscle
      or fight for deserted shacks to hide my nakedness

i will confess i need a little cover

      yet this less solid   more translucent   shabbier habit(at)
      i make
look
      replicates in (admittedly) more muted tones upon a
      flimsier canvas
          the scar collection i so tried to shed

In This Dark Season

what crystals in this white violet
refract like snow
in sun
so flower glitters
cosmetically
on window sill
while all
the ones outdoors
have drooped
under lead breath
of frost

what inner fold
unfurls
within this bulb
to send
for now just speartip
of hope
for a resplendence
peach-blossom
amaryllis

what drives
these cactus
hardly
leaves
spare thorny
seeming tortured
to push forth
as if between
spread thighs
twin buds
that will
like bells
keep
echoing
themselves

December Deeps

     for so long now   so long   so long
our chief star has suffered fatigue

look how he barely drags himself up our high windows
whence he blinded us each morning now empty

at noon on the wind-swept beach light waves goodbye
from waters ready already to frolic flirt on the world's other side

solstice came   solstice went
each day   miser   adds but a minute more before sunset

how do we live   oh   despite all our artifice
how can we live   i ask   in so much without

Inside the Polar Vortex

    far better   need i say it

        to be caught on this side of the translucent window

life outside it
lasts briefly unless
    other than domestic   and even then not without shiver
puff
      extreme   effort

only imitations of life
      these plenteous forms we see as flowers leaves ferns
ice shards reach like tentacles but so indifferent
    reach to capture   devour   not feed on
        all this early

        burning

        light

Dog Reading Ocean Beach

he sniffs
    enchanted with life's detritus thrown by the waves
      with such abandon

    at this post   a warning about what to do and not to do
he springs back
      as if a snake had struck

    in my unknowing
I wonder   coyote fox   scents
    frightened him?   what makes him give this
    post wide berth

    broken armor of horseshoe crabs   such lovely tidbits
      yet this whole dead one
he approaches crouched on his belly   as though life may yet
animate the carapace

for me the beach a play of light on mollusk shards
    a vast occasion for shore birds' ebb-flow dance
for him a history   a chart   as full of meaning
as any mariner's

Fall Clearance

      at sixty-seven
          despite my boneache inwit
             of mortality
i keep buying these discards   summer's leftovers
on a dirty plate
      then seed   bury bulbs   and sticks with roots

    not even for eating or seasoning though for those too

    inside the brain
        something's muscled its way to the reins
something unreasoned   raw   born forever yesterday
    hollering for another spring

Fast Falling

the world is not enough
    with me
each day gives up its grain
to gravity
        leaving the womb   topmost
    more pregnant with its void

below   sand gathers   out of nature
    a pointed cone   ungentled
       no beach plums   nor long grasses

   this dastard ignorance   shrugs even from self-styled
   well-intended
      blowing miasma at us
have not so far stopped gasps before melodies black and white
    played on feathered scales

have not yet turned this ever weakening eye
    from fires incarnadine
       or supremely cold prickpoints in night skies

Punishing Weather

a poppet
a fake   made in china
sold in windowless New Orleans voodoo "museums"

each time the barometer see-saws
like the ball sent up its canal
by hammer's blow at the fair

cosmic forces who know
where i lie   mostly forgotten stick pins through straw brain
stuffed joints that silly bi-valve stitched on my chest

what are they after?
retribution to resound in enormous bodies
oceans   mountains   immeasurables i cannot begin to know

perhaps merely my sins
enormous too   i thought to have hidden
beneath rags and layers of dust

no wonder
those multiple stabbings
        no wonder the fraying   the falling apart

MAN in Nature

       on beach and pond   on woodland trail
disturbances of MAN loom small and large
          tin can bobbing on goldfoil mirror
         discarded tampon   bottle shards
        cigar butt killing seagrass in a circle
dogs bounding   barking growling
       shouts "he's friendly"
worse   misery of friendly's leavings
      deep inside one's boot treads

yes twisted ankle buckled knee just one misstep
make us fervent for human helping hand
    since the nature we so cherish stands assessing
        how soon for gouging juicy eyes
           ripping entrails
       sending a shoot through maze of ribcage

      yet after all
that is the afterall

pause   nature!   assess a second or two more
    that rag-and-bone   that heap
still needs some seasoning some breaking of the bonds

OFTEN FANGED LIGHT

    for   when animated
worse than plastic waste it held a mess of wrongs

    such wordless outrage shut in such small selves
    such griefs no tenderest mother could allay
    such scars   such weeping silent wounds
    such deadly blows to all that lives

    how soon is safe dispersal for redemption?

Wake

boat
I am laden with silver gasps and groans
pursued
above around
by winged ghosts
gently feathered
yet not at all given to quietness

were I attentive only
to their calls
tempted
I'd turn my bow
toward limitless horizons
never to fit again
into this o so narrow jostled segmented harbor

throw overboard my rainbow rows
of small deaths to the breathing
whence I snagged them
follow them
as they in a last languor
spiral
to that deep sky
where only life
sheds luminescences

Gratitude

      third week in august   a day rare as black pearls
my eyes leak
          not with salt spray

i'm twenty-four years older than you   father
   when you stopped drawing breath

yet every motion of these aging limbs
         through gently heaving waters
is what you taught me
     and the spur
          go go farther   till   at large

   this coast
      like wings of damselflies
        varied   astonishing in strength
      though living for a day
        this black-pearl day

you my mother   who left me much too soon
handed me the inner ticking clock
    make your life now now now where body and soul may
       despite the thousand shocks
breathe
   on such rare days
together

Avis Semper Rara

      not Leonardo's lines   desire more taut   than Lisa's smile
          nor Wright nor Boeing
catch   unfolding
     the stretch three times the size
        armed grace
           burst that mere eye can barely apprehend
our heavy poison-spewing machines so try to emulate

    not just those rafts on thermal air baths
        yellow iris fixed
           voices sounding weak as if themselves the prey
but air-sleek body balanced on stilts
    sword whose tip outdoes pincers on the surgeon's tray
catch
     wriggles   limp giving up   the fight
       of all that too wants life

    not a one   not one
flaunts
    what poor selves only yearn for
       that *sprezzatura*
          against the pull of dirt

In Darkest Hours

true   solstice awaits   around this month's corner

the young point to the calendar   there   there
     there   will be light again

not all of us who've tunneled through darkness time and again
will wrestle with Pandora's escapees once more
not all of us will win

let us then   whatever's left of love   let us
walk by this changing shore
let us not cling   or hold hands only   or try
     mere stitches on this rip of howling night

let us   whatever's left of love   let us
with scalpels   jaws of life   solder guns
let us
cut   break apart   scrape   discard
then begin if we can the delicate   unforgiving   work
     whose end we shall not see

     mending the broken shards
          this struggling light

Acknowledgments

"Coming to Light." "If You're Not There All Along."
    Dragon Poetry Review. (Summer, 2018).
"Snailing to Byzantium." *Adelaide*. (Spring, 2018).
"Unrest of Migrant Selves." *Adelaide*. (Spring, 2018).
"Encryption." *Muddy River Poetry Review*. (Spring, 2018).
"as date approaches." *Fourth & Sycamore* (November, 2017).
"Kitchen Window Still Life." *Fourth & Sycamore Literary
    Journal* (October, 2016).
"Fall Clearance." *Dragon Poetry Review* (Summer, 2016).
"This Last Day of August." *Dragon Poetry Review*
    (Summer, 2016).
"A Lot More than Half Way." *Pyrokinection* (Spring, 2016).
"Amphibian Landings." *Wilderness House Literary Review*
    (Spring, 2016).
"Cleansing the Haunted House." *Lost Coast Review* 6, 2
    (Winter 2015).
"December Deeps." *Wilderness House Literary Review*
    (Spring, 2016).
"January's Small Mercies." *Muddy River Poetry Review*
    (Spring, 2016).
"Love Poem to the L(ibrary) Before IT." *Bangalore Review* I,
    10. (March, 2014).
"Opal Moon." *Circleshow Journal*, 11. (Feb., 2015).
"Virtual Spaces." *Muddy River Poetry Review*. (Spring, 2016).
"Paris Sediments." *CircleShow Journal*, (Winter, 2012-13).

"Wake." *Ginosko Literary Journal* (Summer, 2008).
"In This Dark Season," *Terrain.: A Journal of the Built & Natural Environments* (Summer, 2007).
"Beach Tales." *The Larcom Review*, 1 (1999).

About the Author

Born in Romania, Anca Vlasopolos became a UN refugee in 1962 and with her mother immigrated to the United States in 1963. She is professor emerita of English and Comparative Literature (Wayne State University). After being a longtime resident of the Detroit area in Michigan, she now resides with her husband, writer Anthony Ambrogio, on Cape Cod, Massachusetts.

She has published *Cartographies of Scale (and Wing)* (Avignon Press, 2015); *The New Bedford Samurai* (Twilight Times Books, 2007)—recipient of the Wayne State University Board of Governors Award; *Penguins in a Warming World* (Ragged Sky Press, 2007)—three poems nominated for a Pushcart Award; *No Return Address: A Memoir of Displacement* (Columbia University Press, 2000), awarded the YMCA Writer's Voice Grant for Creative Non-Fiction in 2001, and the Wayne State University Board of Governors Award and the Arts Achievement Award in 2002; a poetry e-chapbook, *Sidereal and Closer Griefs* (www.origamicondom.org); chapbooks *Through the Straits, at Large* and *The Evidence of Spring*; and a detective novel, *Missing Members* (trans. *Miembros Ausentes*); as well as nearly three hundred poems and short stories; a libretto for an opera, *Keanu and the Magic Coals*, performed by the Michigan Opera Theater and the Hilberry Theater; *Arts at an Exhibition* and *The Poetry Harmonium,* music and poetry compact-disc collaboration with composer Christian Kreipke. She was associate editor of *Corridors Literary Magazine.* She has also published a book of literary criticism, *The Symbolic Method of Coleridge, Baudelaire, and Yeats*, and over thirty scholarly articles and book chapters on literature and the environment, feminist theory, eugenics in literature, film, and theater.

www.ingramcontent.com/pod-product-compliance
Lightning Source LLC
Chambersburg PA
CBHW021201100426
42735CB00046B/799